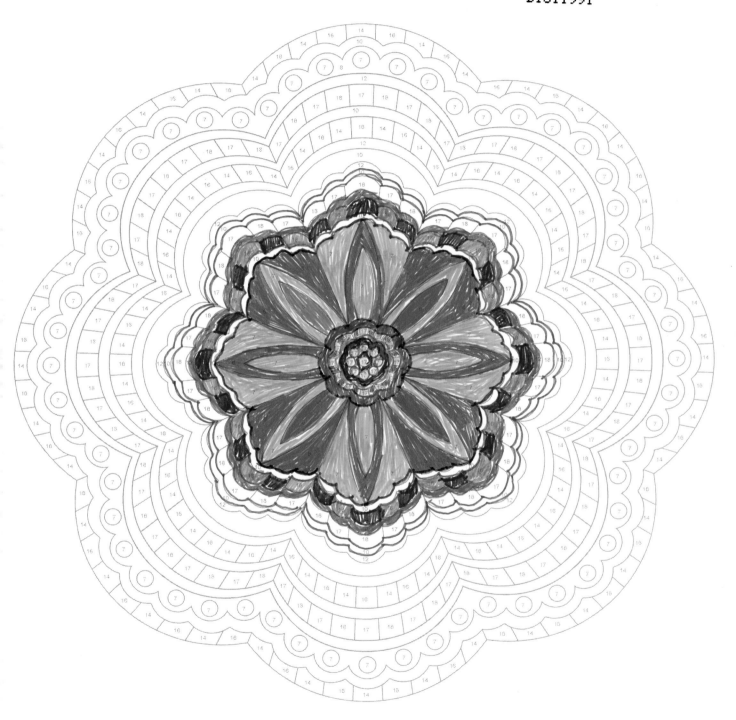

MANDALAS

COLOR BY NUMBER COLORING BOOK

SHALA KERRIGAN

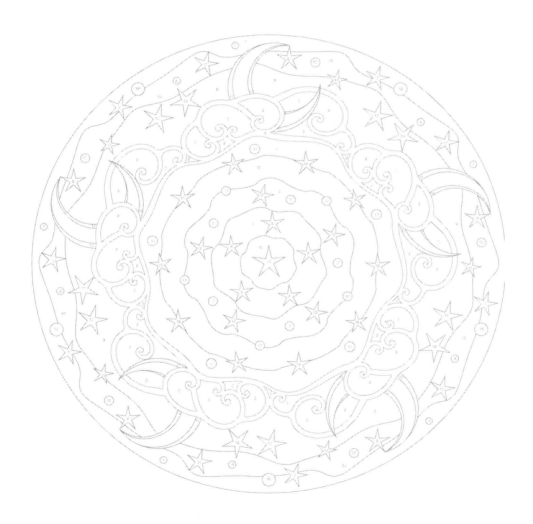

DOVER PUBLICATIONS, INC.
MINEOLA, NEW YORK

Bibliographical Note

Mandalas Color by Number Coloring Book is a new work,
first published by Dover Publications, Inc., in 2015.

International Standard Book Number

ISBN-13: 978-0-486-79797-7
ISBN-10: 0-486-79797-X

Manufactured in the United States by LSC Communications
79797X11   2019
www.doverpublications.com

This coloring collection features forty-six full-page mandala designs for you to color. Each plate is shown in full-color on the inside covers. You can duplicate these images simply by following the color guide found on the inside front cover, or choose your own colors for a more personal touch. As part of Dover's *Creative Haven* series for the experienced colorist, each plate is highly detailed, perfect for experimentation with color and technique. Plus, the perforated, unbacked pages allow you to choose any media you like, and make displaying your work easy!

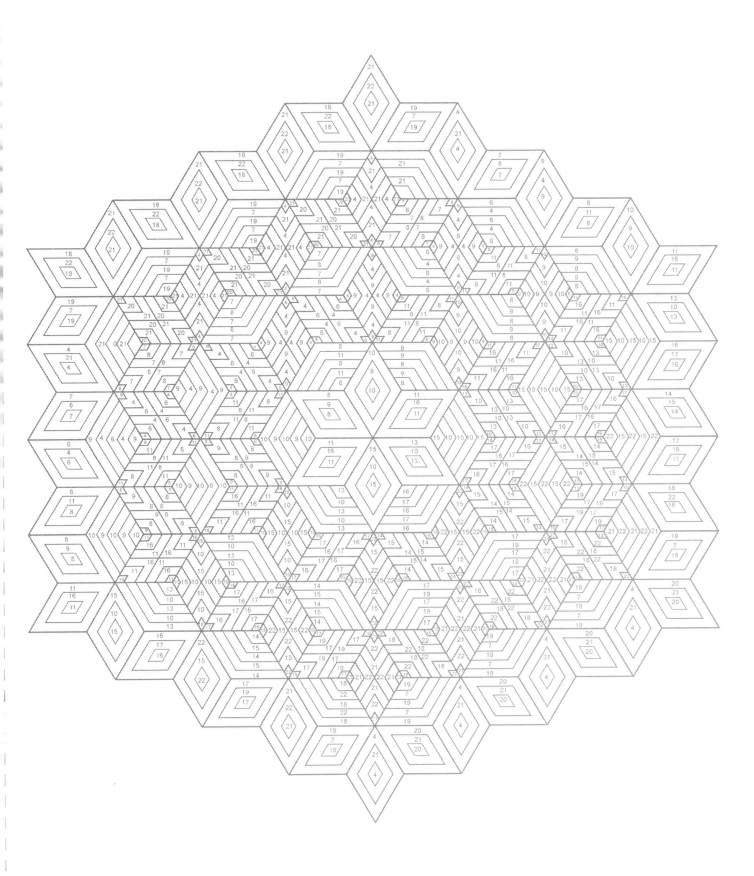

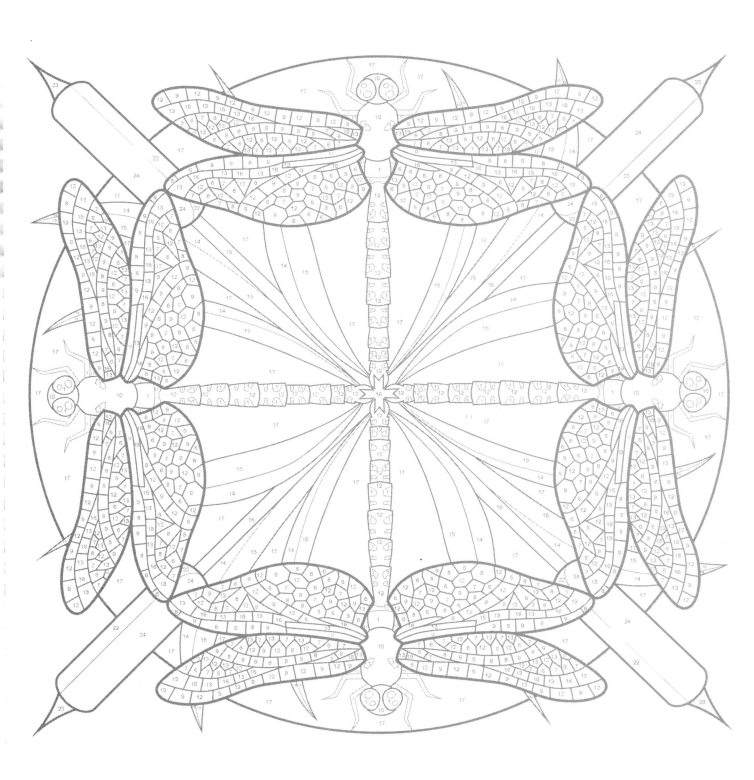

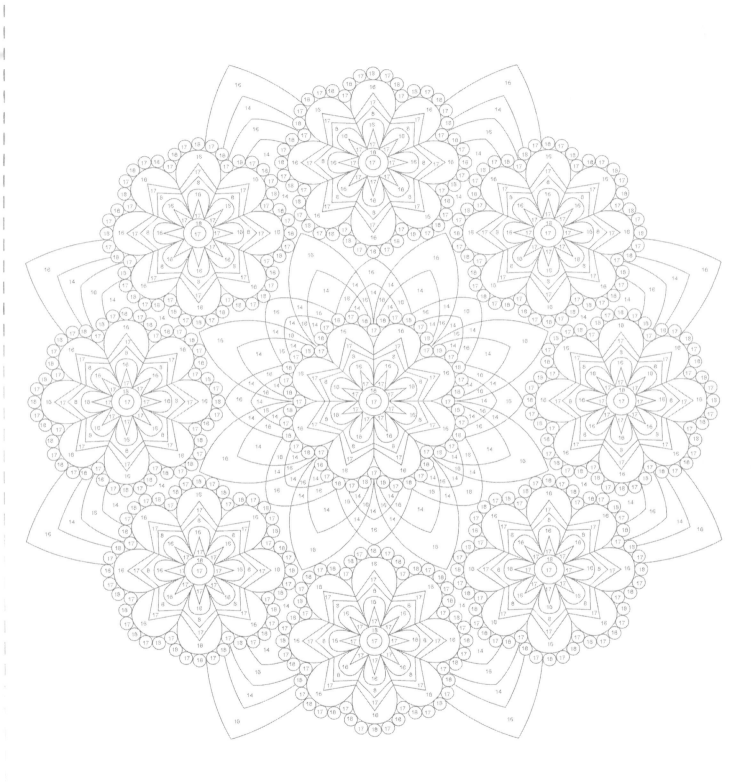

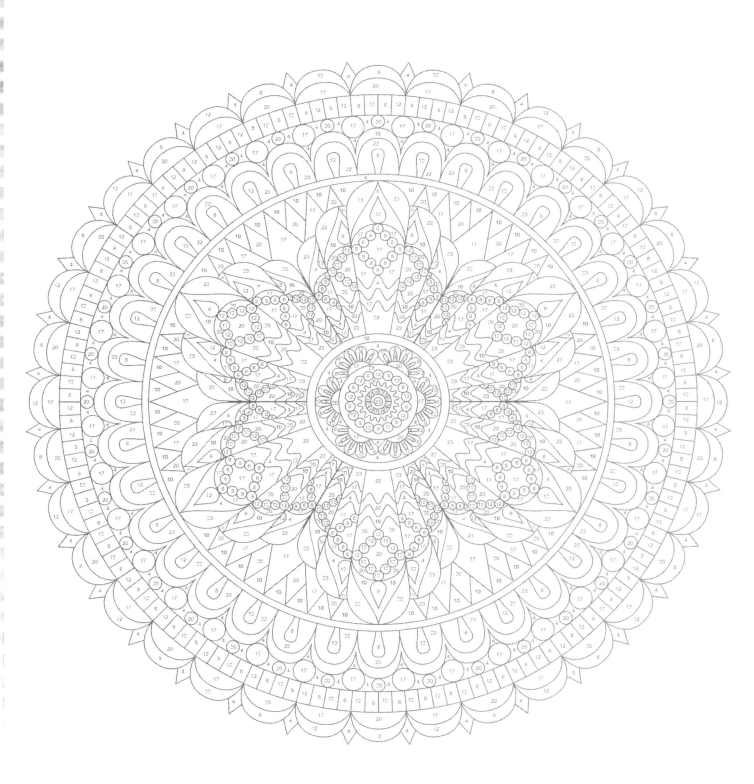

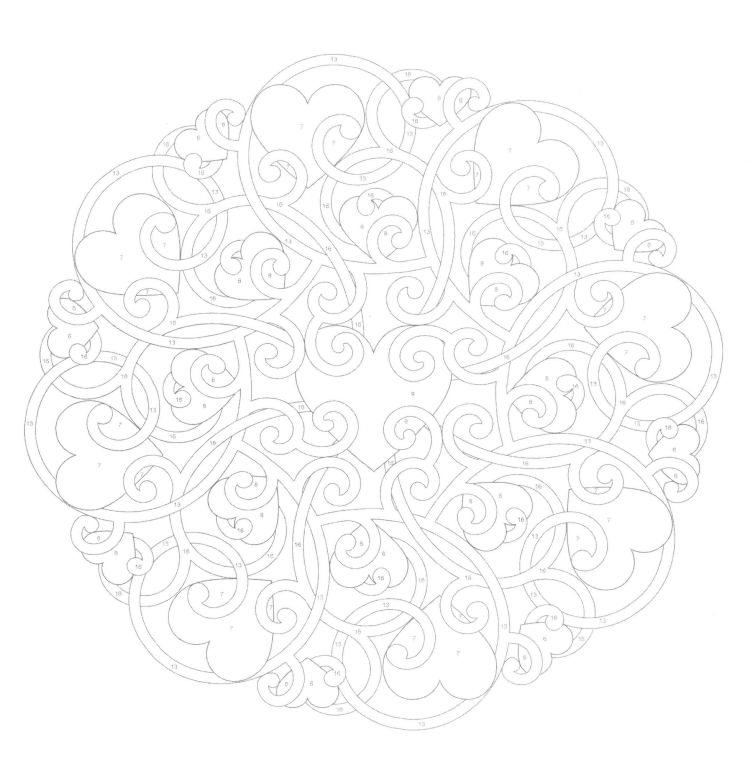

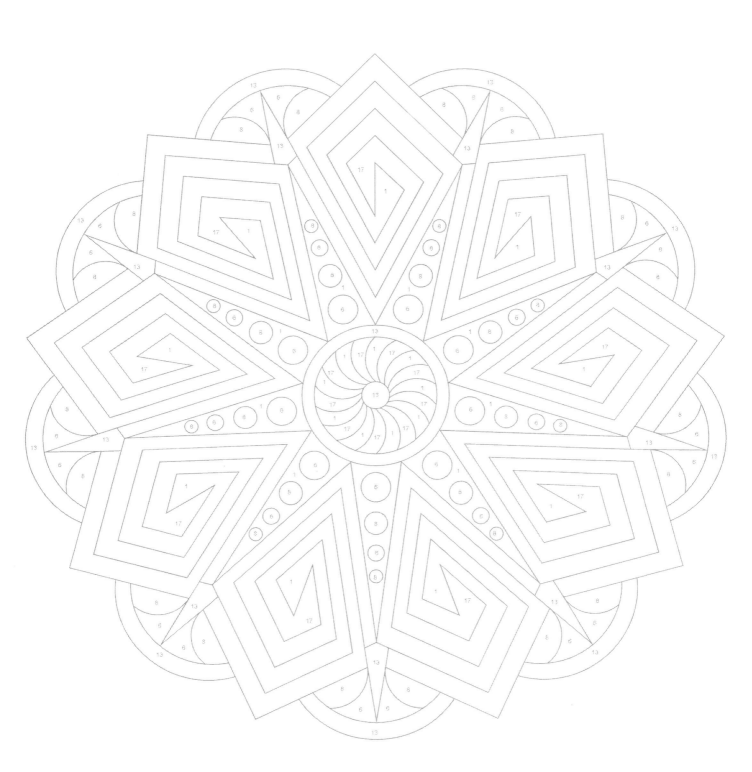

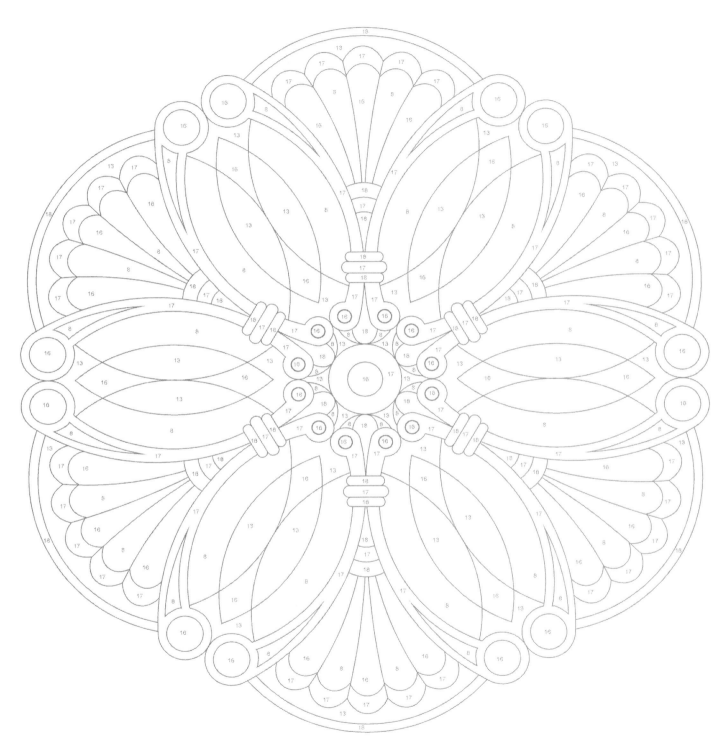

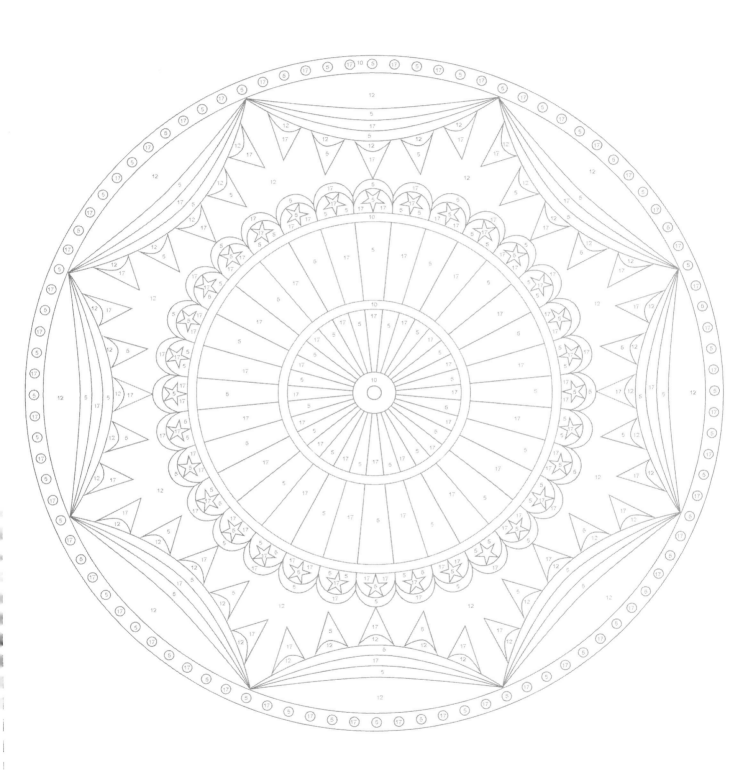

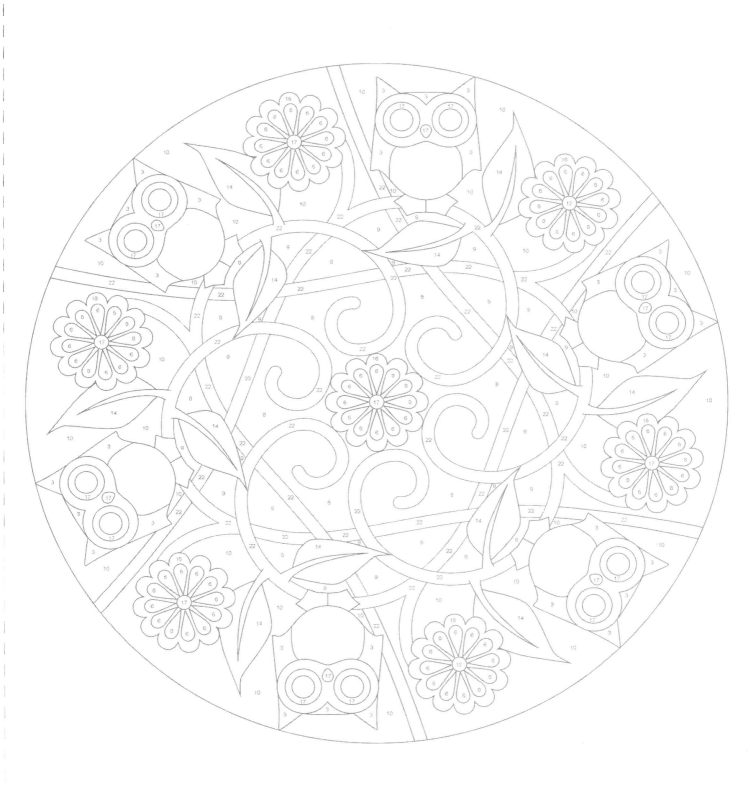

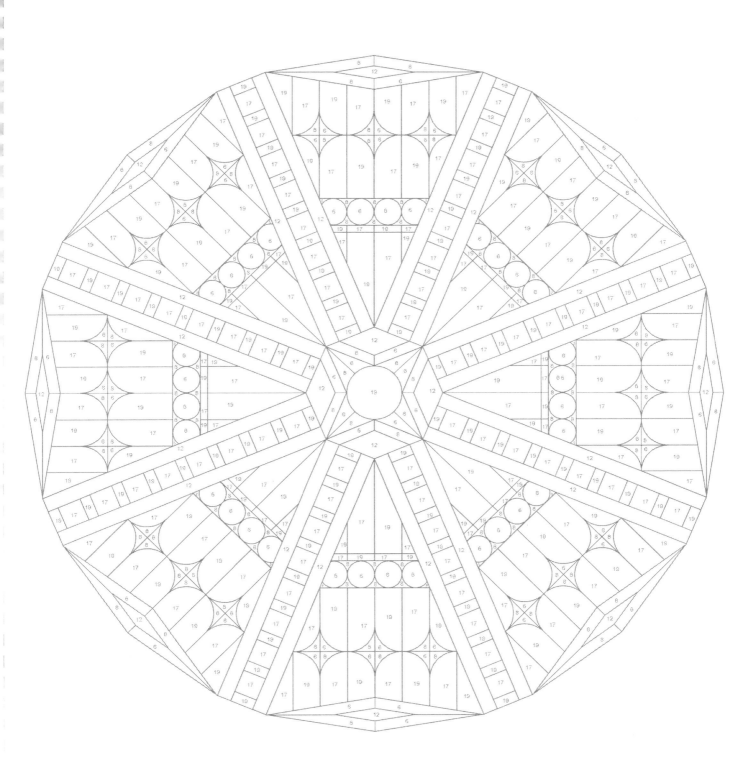

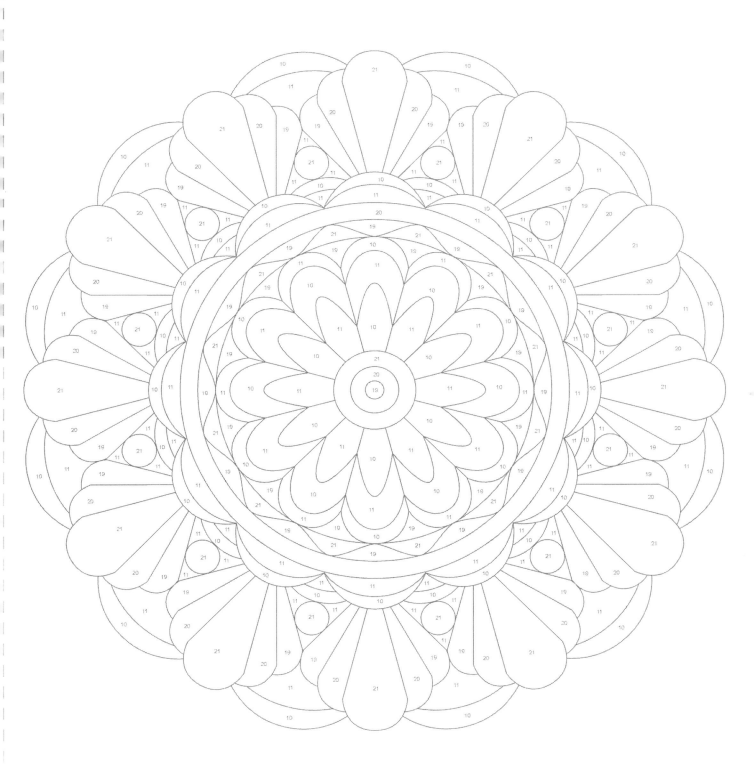

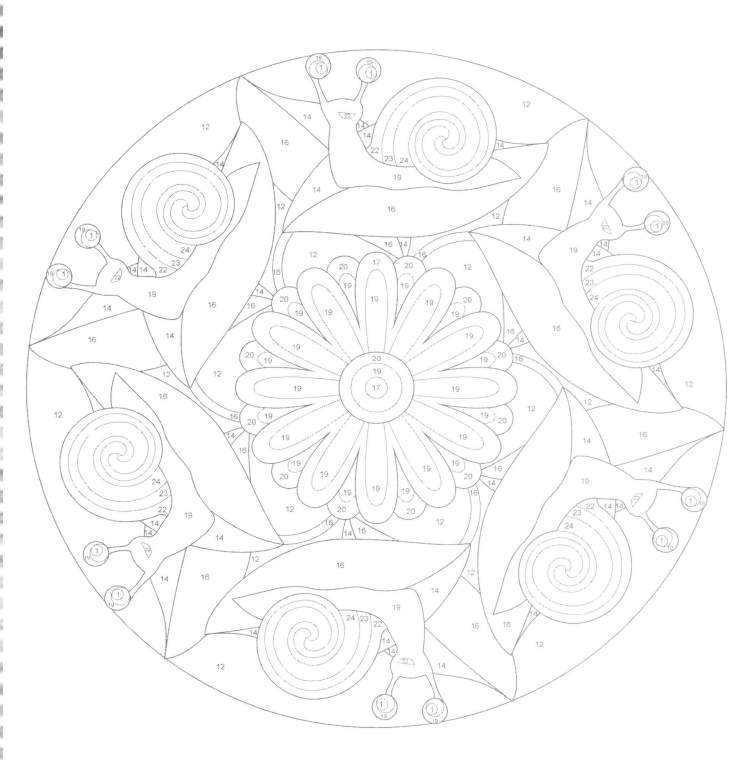

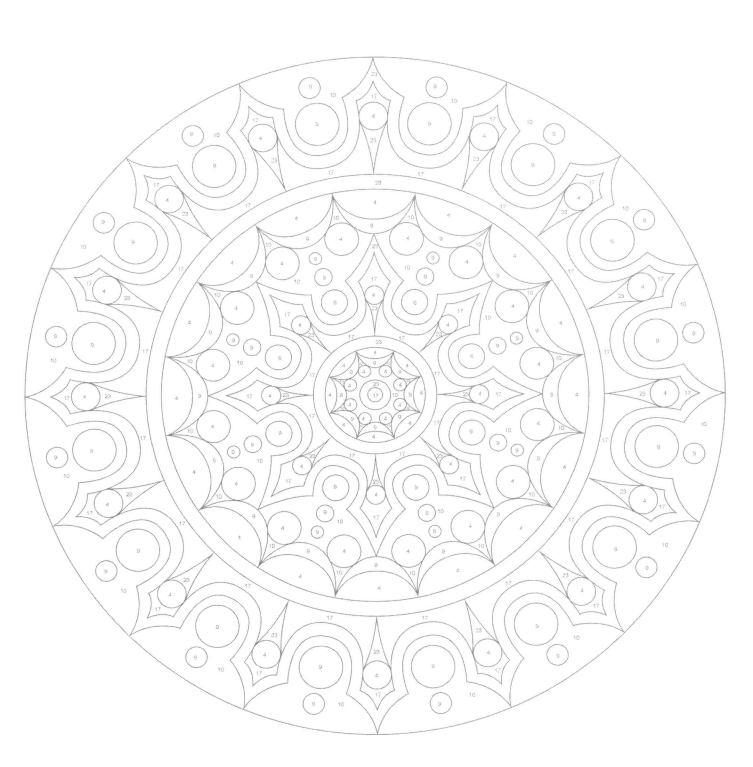

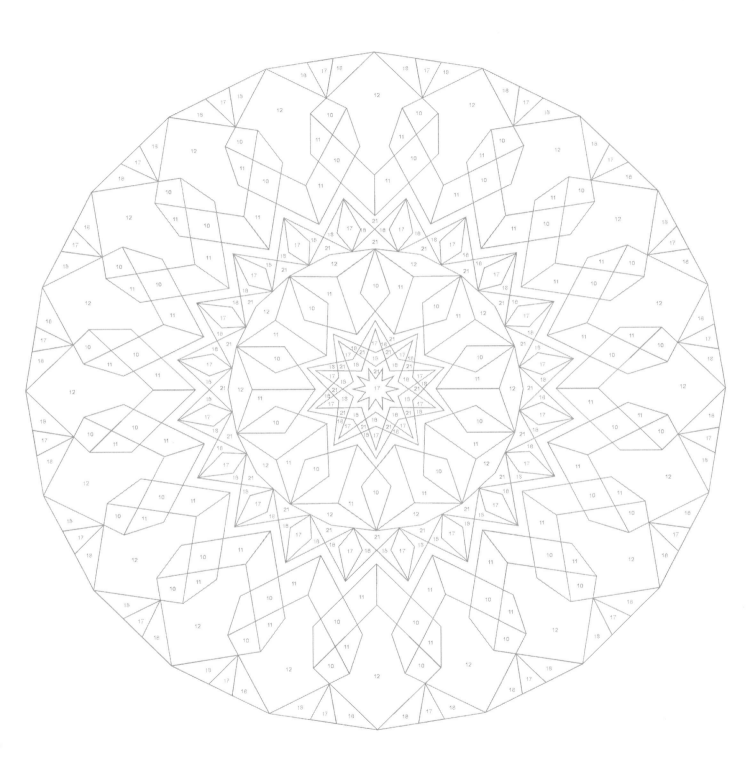

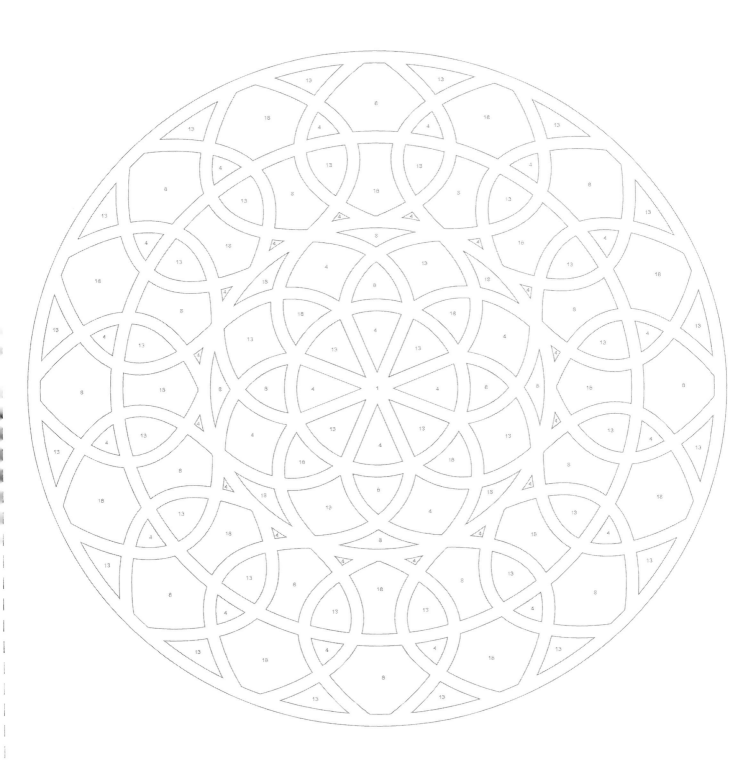

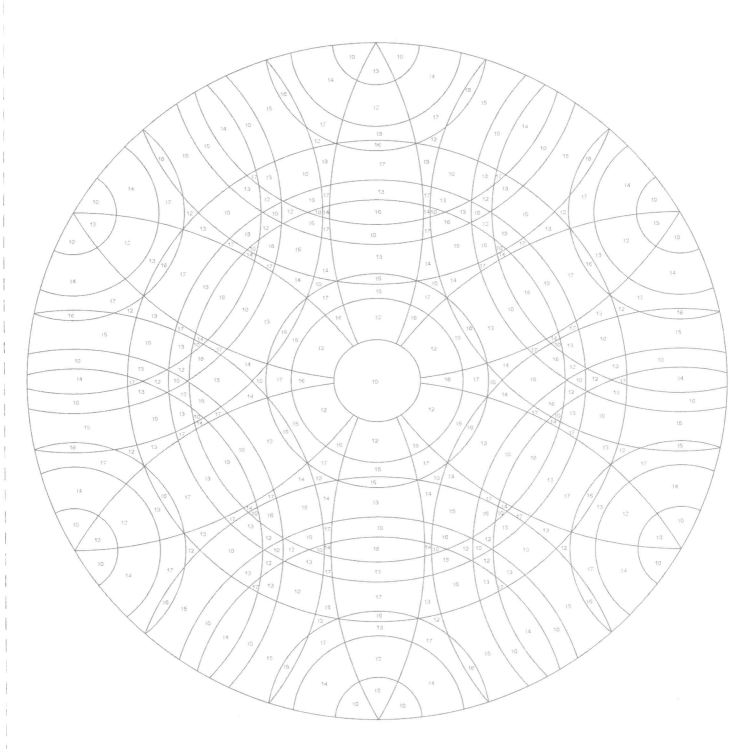

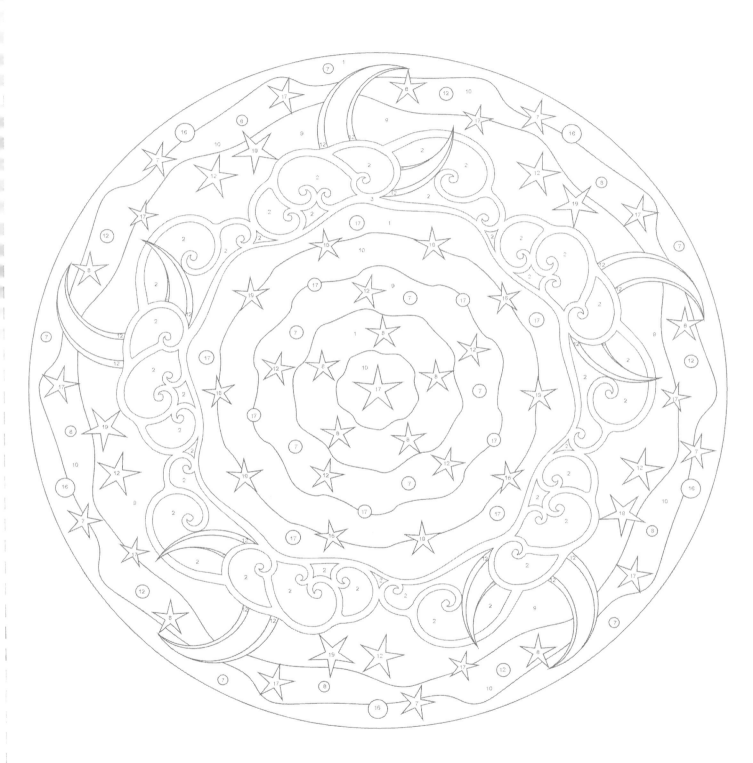

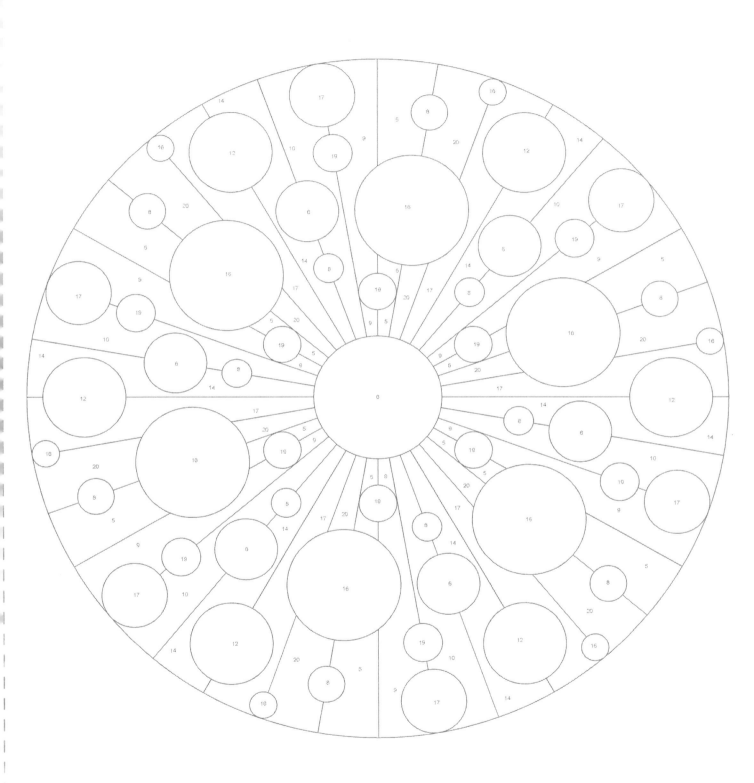

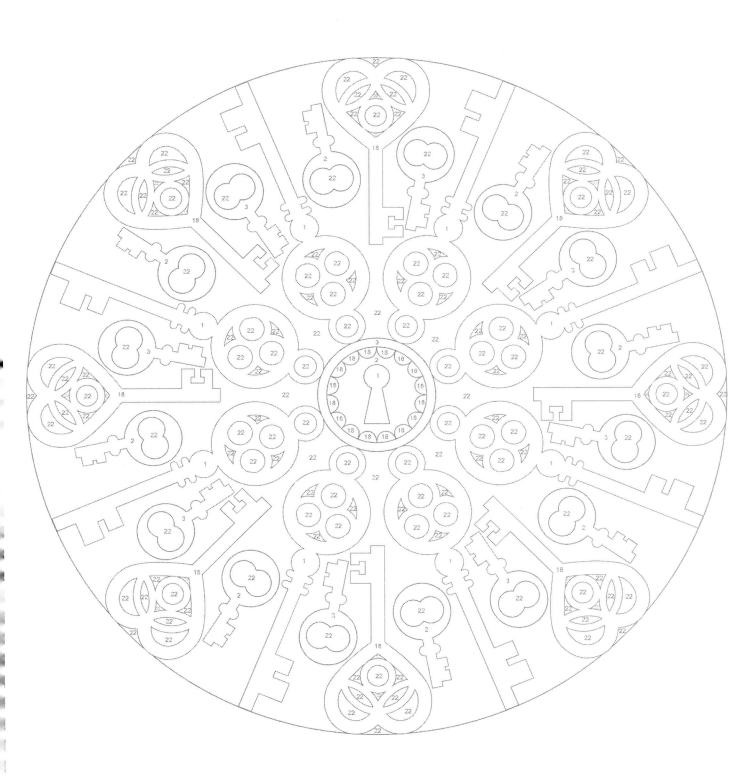

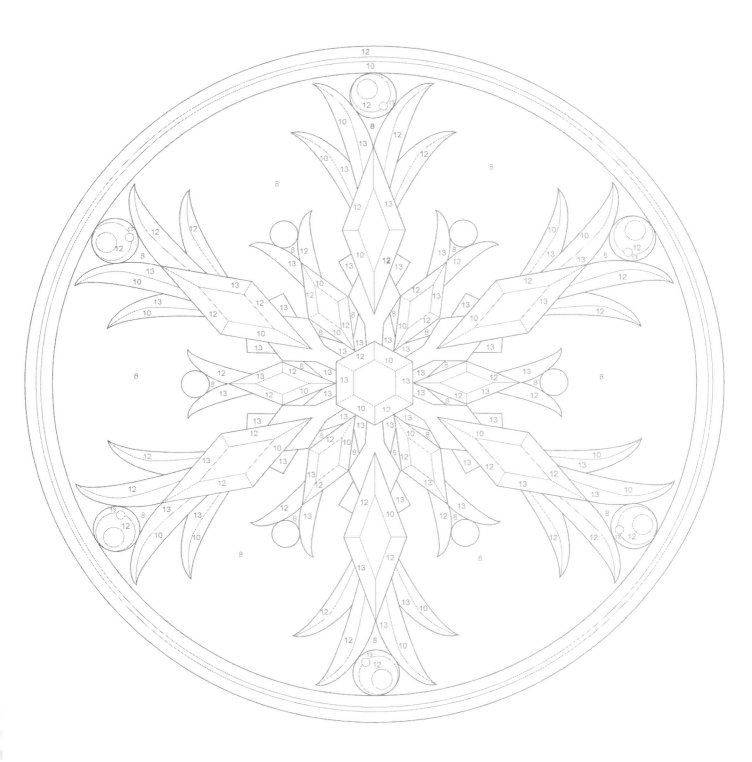

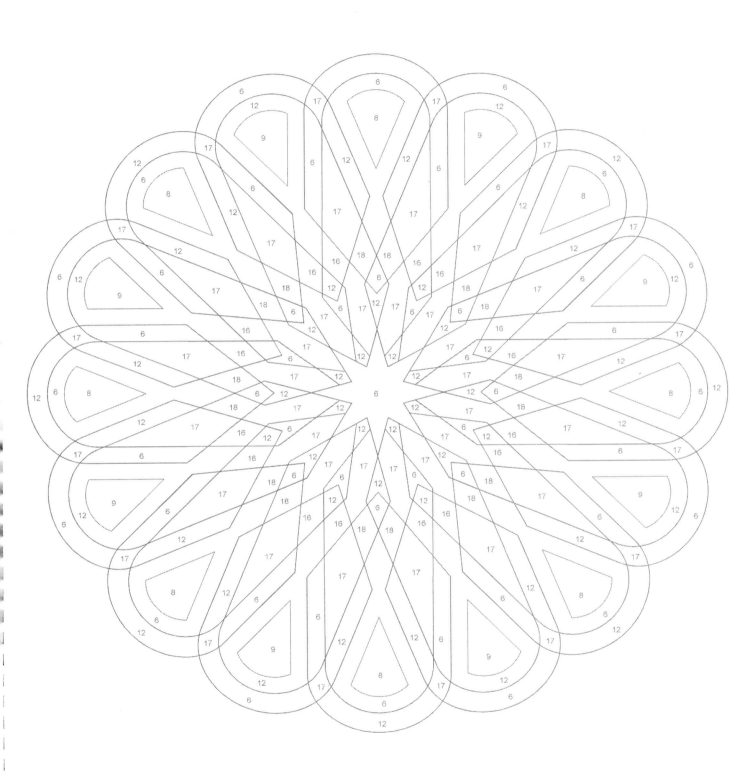

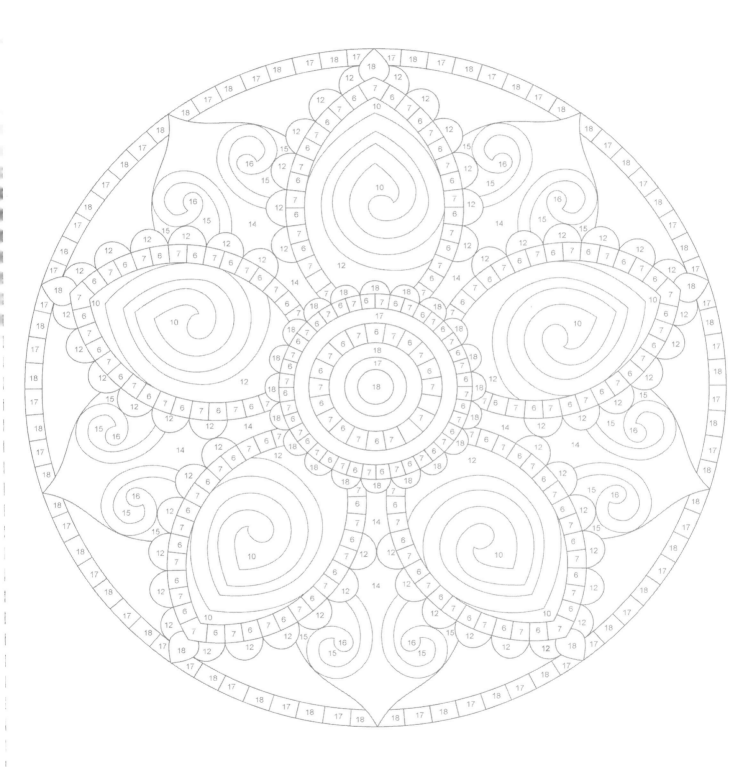

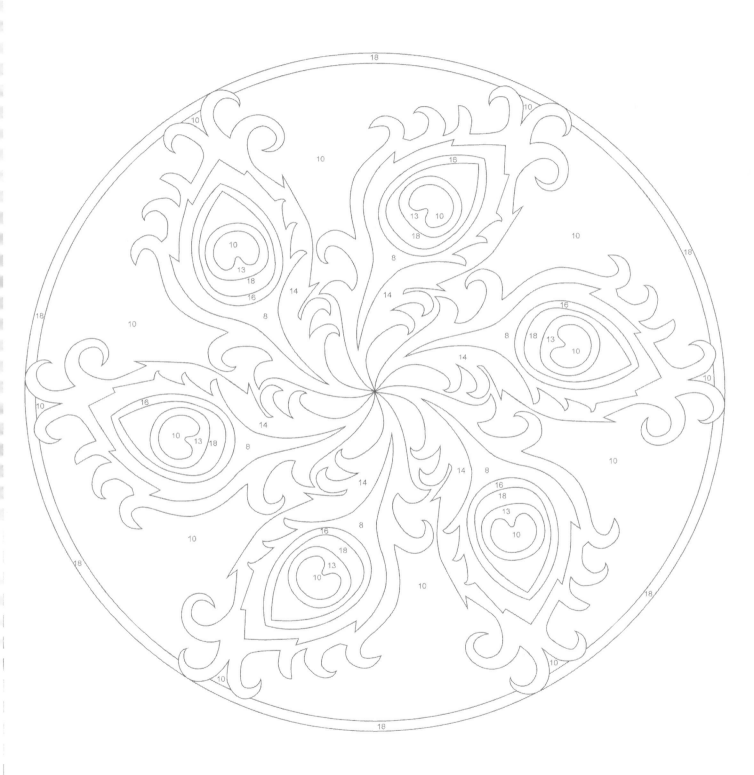

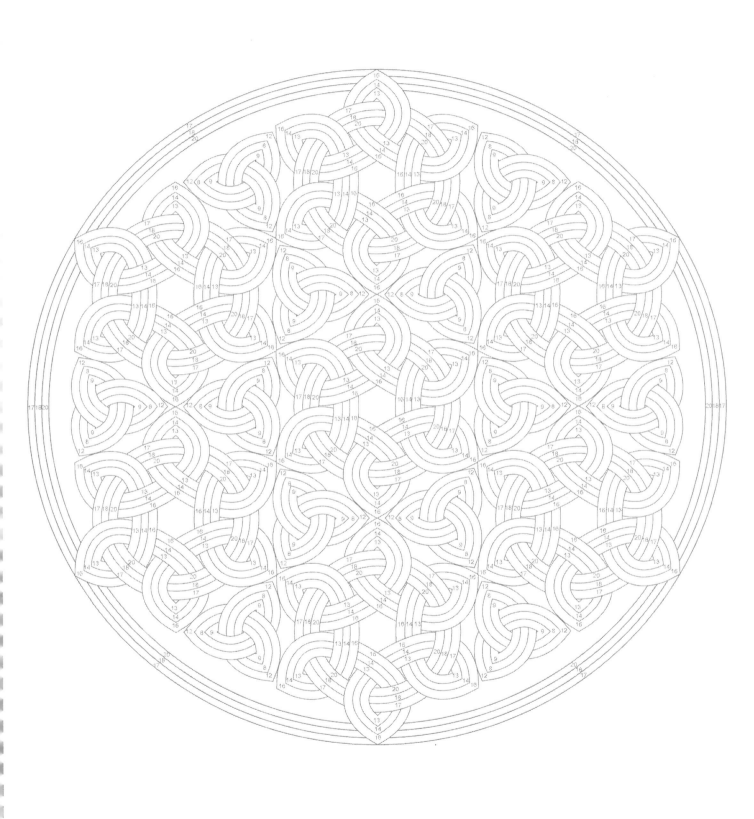

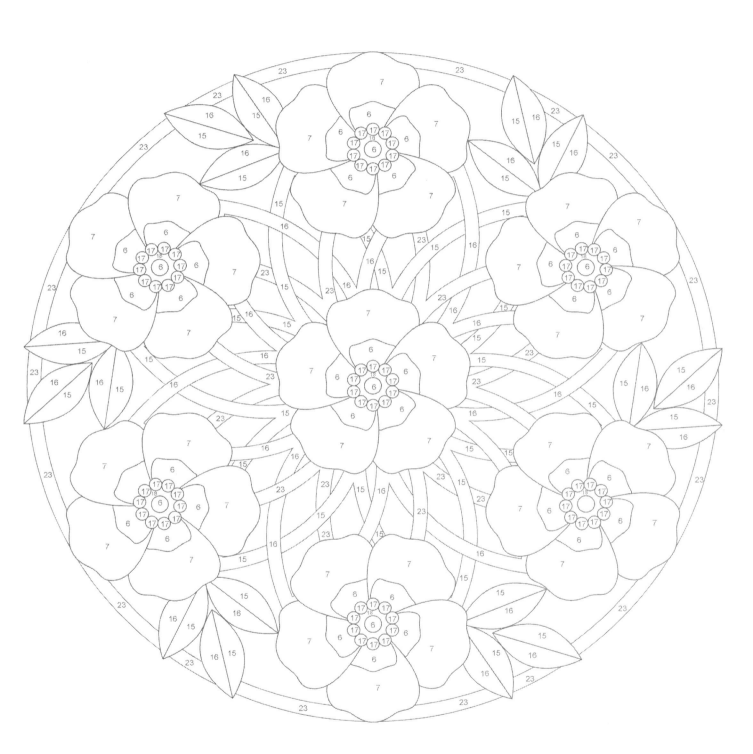

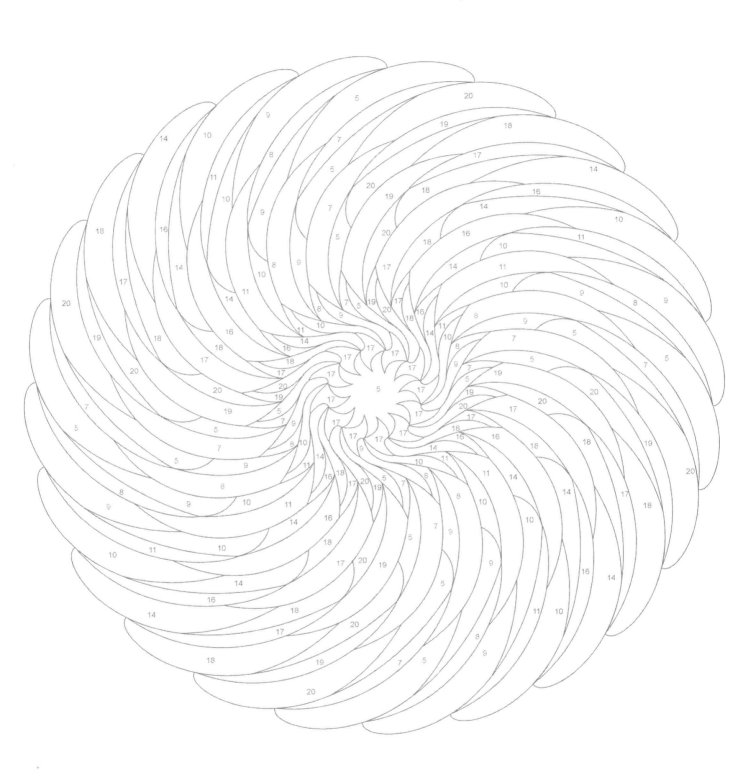

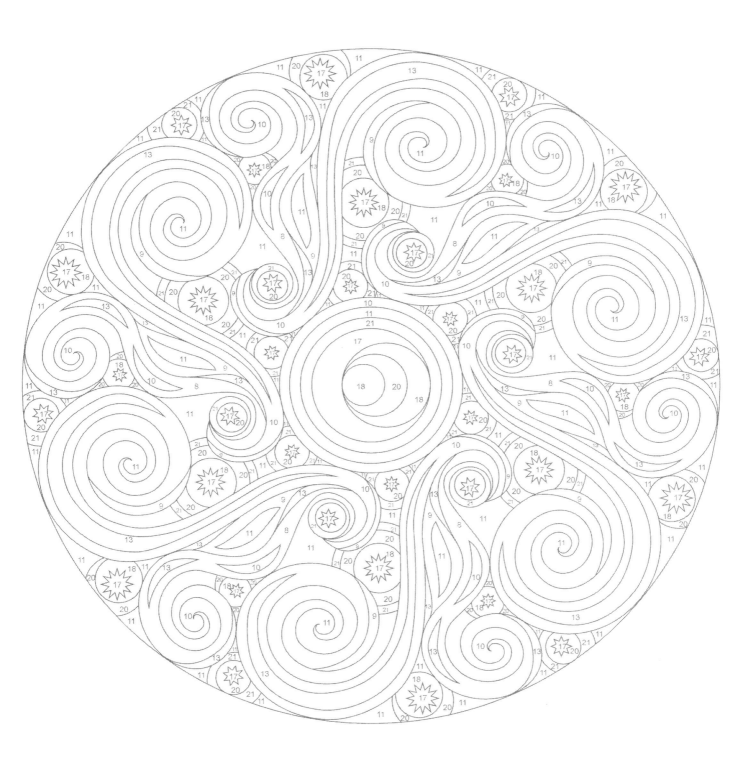

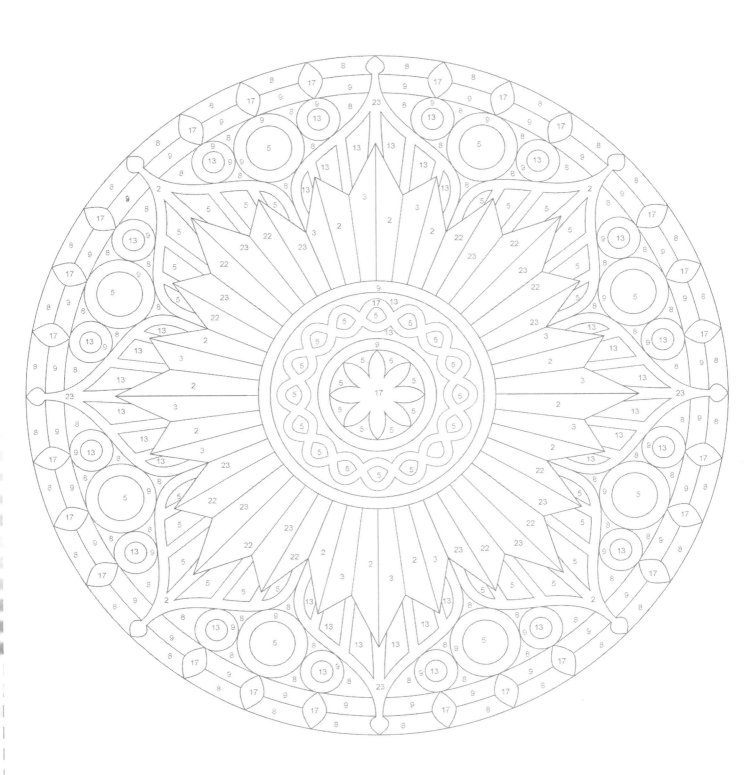

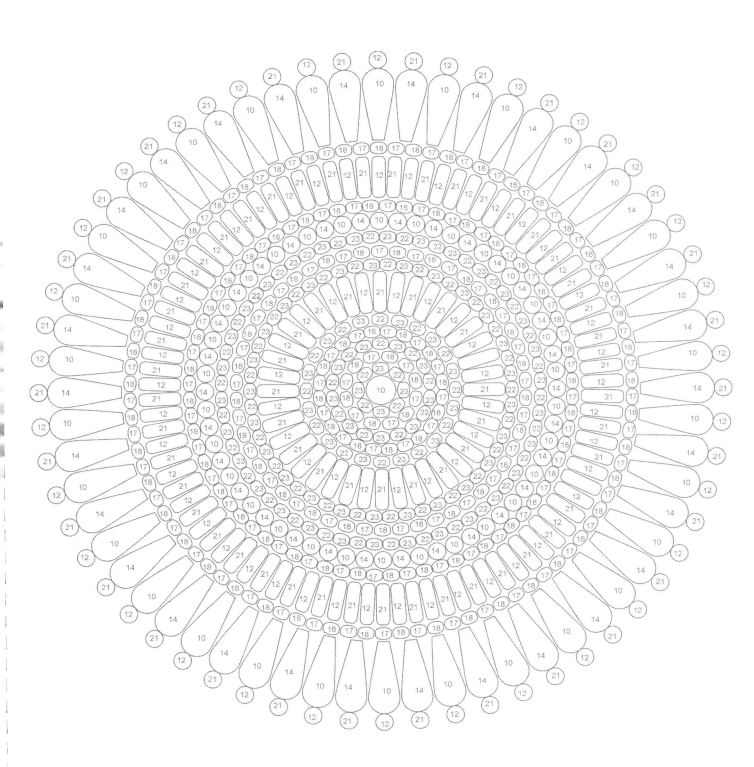

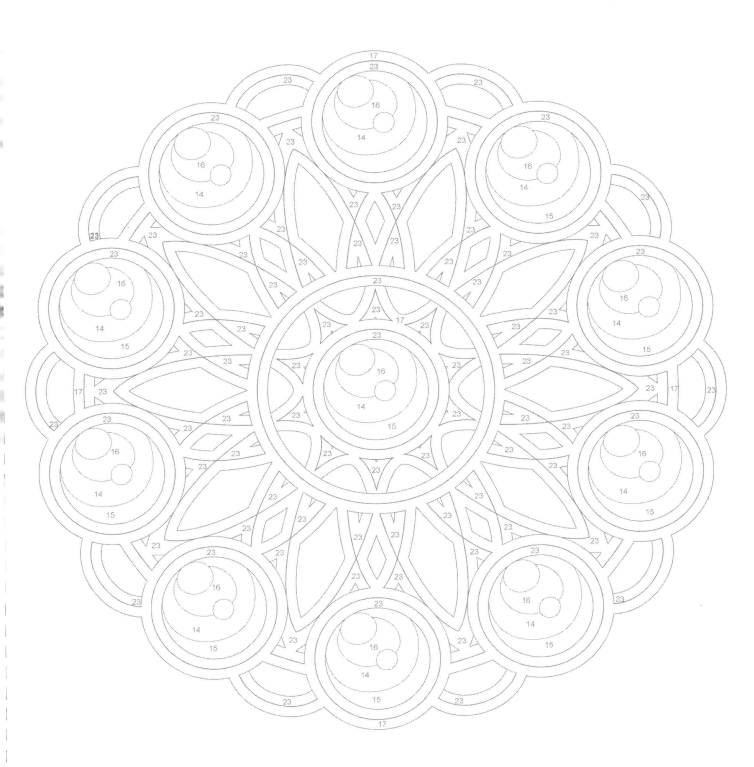

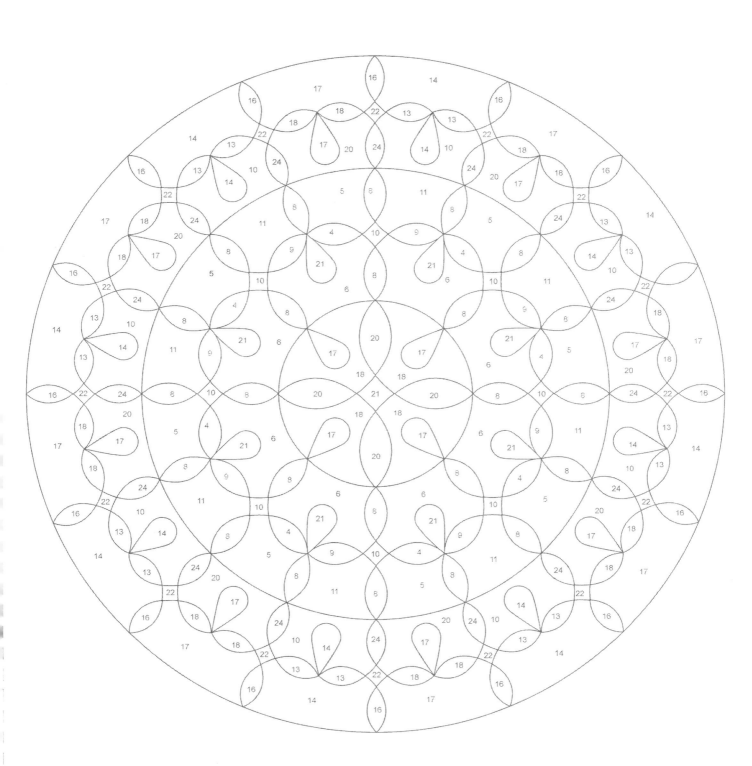

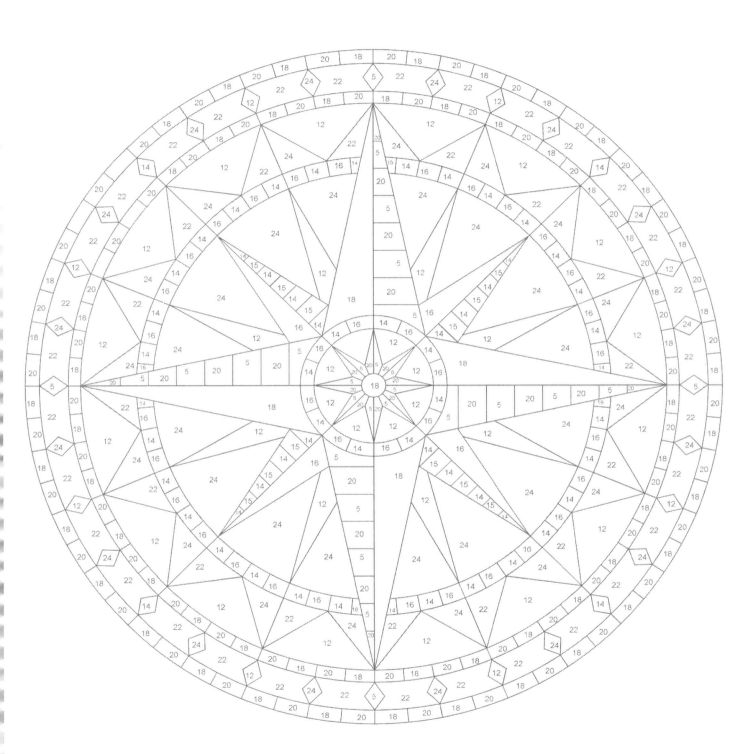

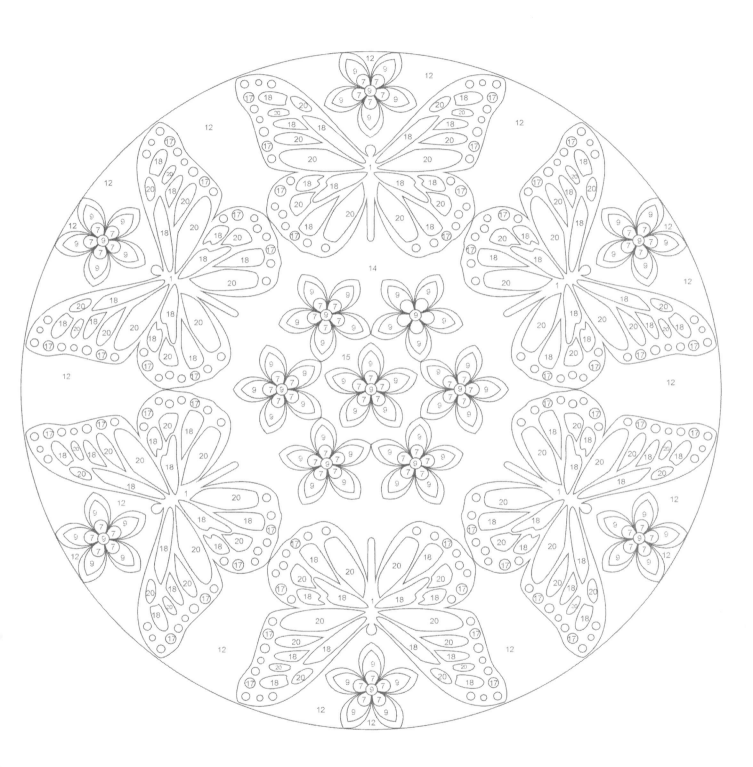

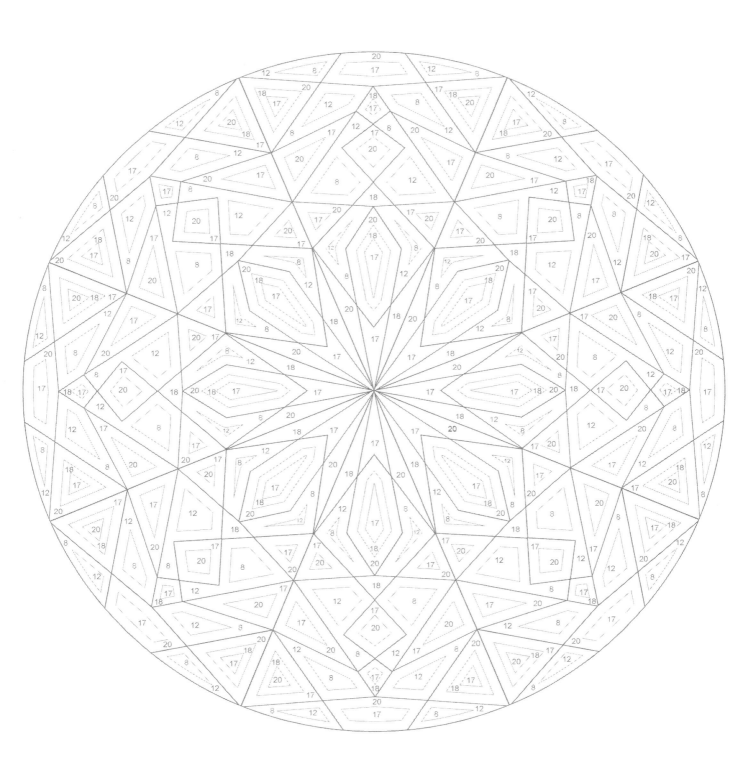

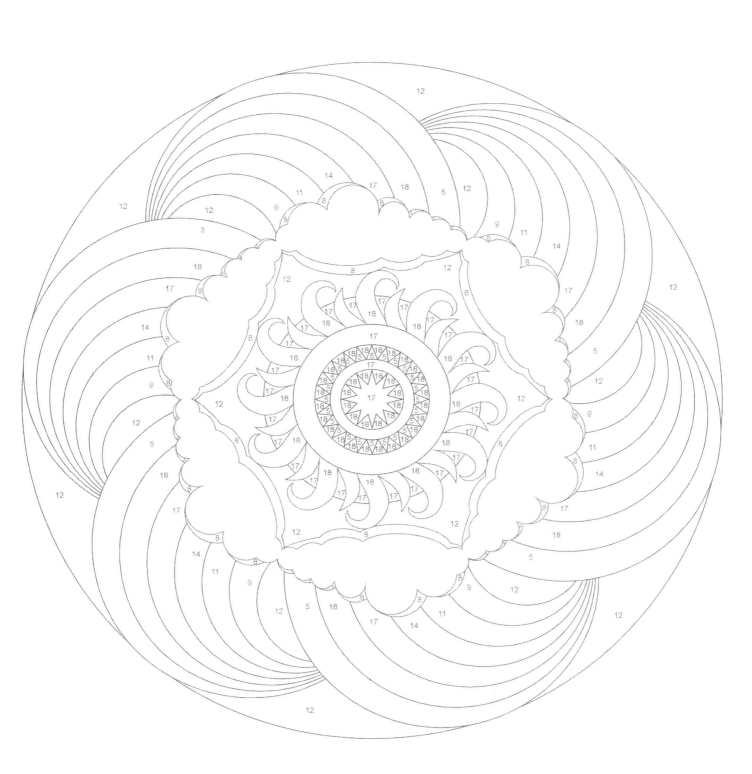

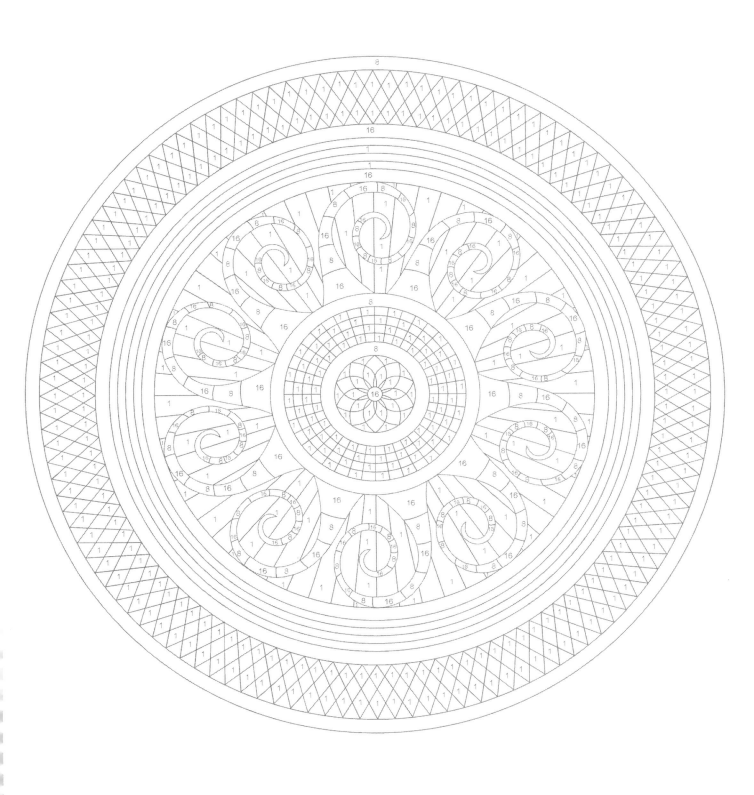

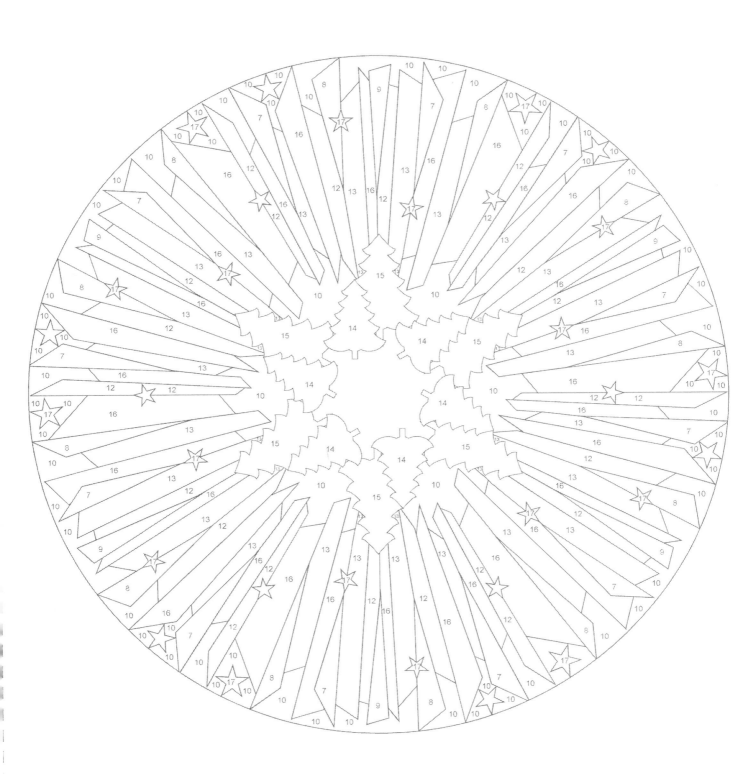

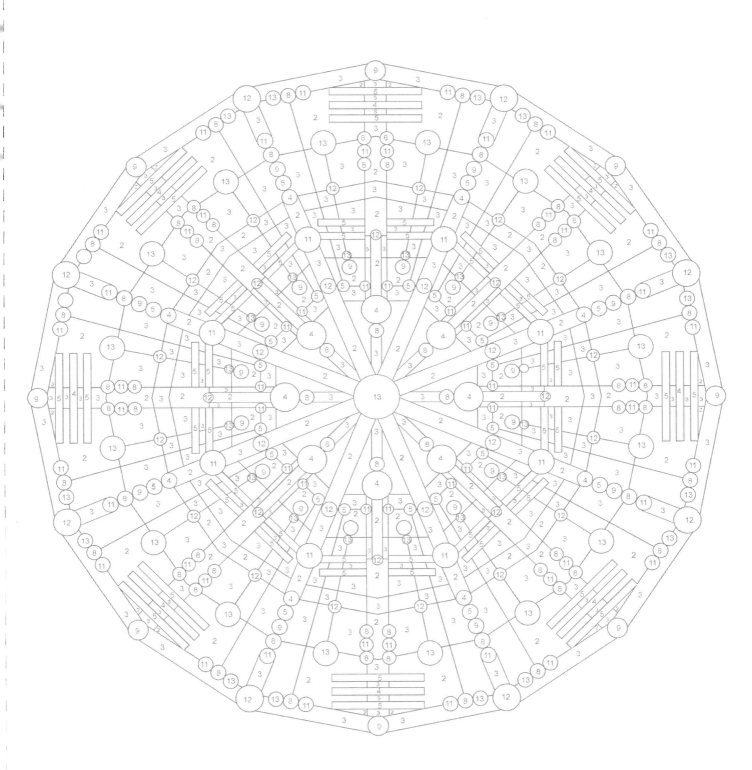

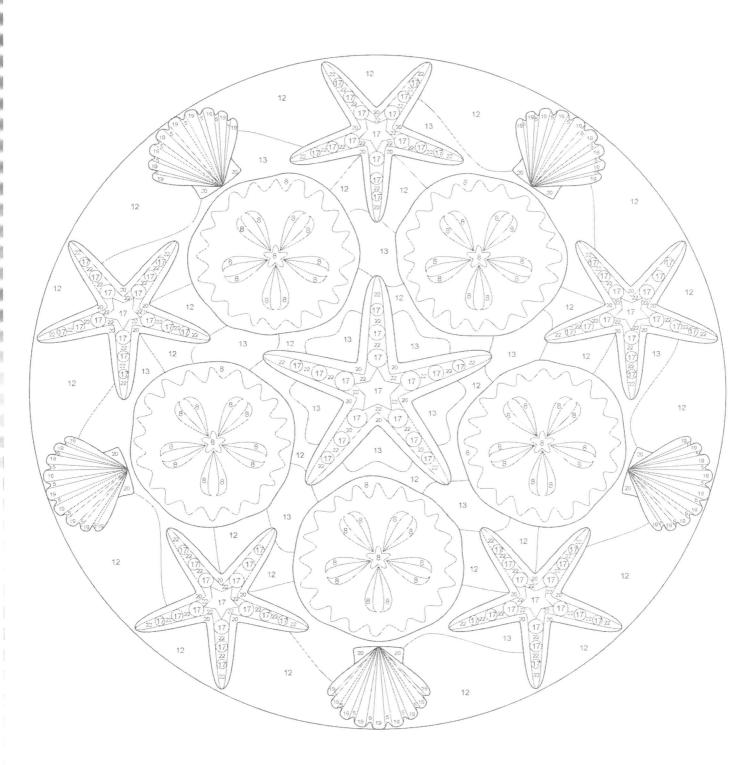

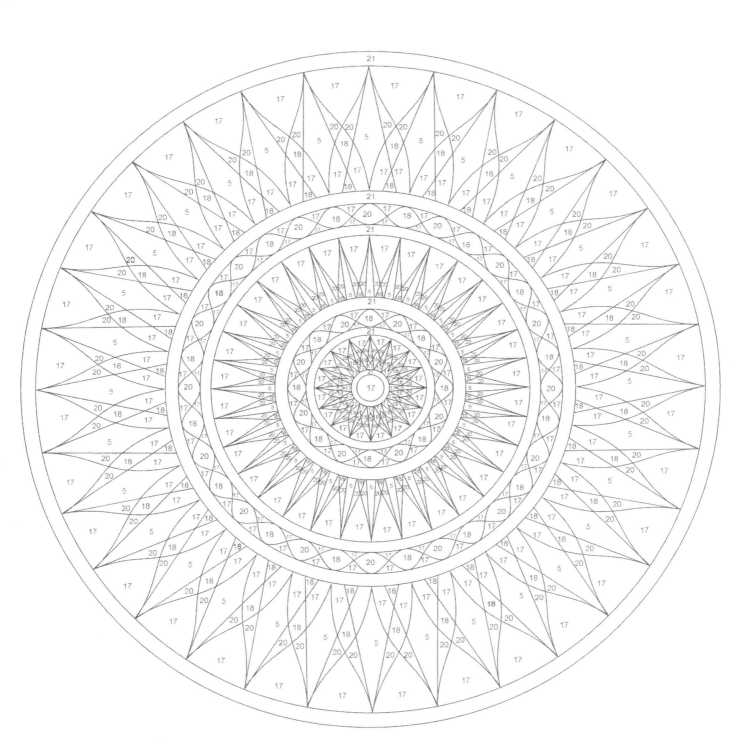